ASTROLOGY
SELF-CARE

Pisces

ASTROLOGY SELF-CARE

Pisces

Live your best life by the stars

Sarah Bartlett

First published in Great Britain in 2022 by Yellow Kite
An imprint of Hodder & Stoughton
An Hachette UK company

1

A CIP catalogue record for this title is
available from the British Library

Hardback ISBN 978 1 399 70491 5
eBook ISBN 978 1 399 70493 9
Audiobook ISBN 978 1 399 70492 2

Designed by Goldust Design

Typeset in Nocturne Serif by Hewer Text UK Ltd, Edinburgh
Printed and bound in Great Britain by Clays Ltd, Elcograf S.p.A.

Hodder & Stoughton policy is to use papers that are
natural, renewable and recyclable products and made
from wood grown in sustainable forests. The logging and
manufacturing processes are expected to conform to the
environmental regulations of the country of origin.

Yellow Kite
Hodder & Stoughton Ltd
Carmelite House
50 Victoria Embankment
London EC4Y 0DZ

www.yellowkitebooks.co.uk

Believe in yourself. Believe in your dreams.
If you don't, who will?

Jon Bon Jovi, American singer–songwriter

There is a path, hidden between the road of reason and the hedgerow of dreams, which leads to the secret garden of self-knowledge. This book will show you the way.

Contents

Introduction

The ancient Greek goddess Gaia arose from Chaos and was the personification of the Earth and all of Nature. One of the first primordial beings, along with Tartarus (the Underworld), Eros (love) and Nyx (night), as mother of all life, she is both the embodiment of all that this planet is and its spiritual caretaker.

It's hardly likely you will want to become a full-time Mother Earth, but many of us right now are caring more about our beautiful planet and all that lives upon it. To nurture and respect this amazing place we call home, and to preserve this tiny dot in the Universe, the best place to start is, well, with you.

Self-care is about respecting and honouring who you are as an individual. It's about realising that nurturing yourself is neither vanity nor a conceit, but a creative act that brings an awesome sense of awareness and a deeper connection to the Universe and all that's in it. Caring about yourself means you care about everything in the cosmos – because you are part of it.

But self-care isn't just about trekking to the gym, jogging around the park or eating the right foods. It's also about discovering who you are becoming as an individual and caring for that authenticity (and loving and caring about who we are becoming means others can love and care about us, too). This is where the art of sun-sign astrology comes in.

Astrology and Self-Care

So what is astrology? And how can it direct each of us to the right self-care pathway? Put simply, astrology is the study of the planets, sun and moon and their influence on events and people here on Earth. It is an art that has been used for thousands of years to forecast world events, military and political outcomes and, more recently, financial market trends. As such, it is an invaluable tool for understanding our own individuality and how to be true to ourselves. Although there is still dispute within astrological circles as to whether the planets actually physically affect us, there is strong evidence to show that the cycles and patterns they create in the sky have a direct mirroring effect on what happens down here on Earth and, more importantly, on each individual's personality.

Your horoscope or birth-chart is a snapshot of the planets, sun and moon in the sky at the moment you were born. This amazing picture reveals all your innate potential, characteristics and qualities. In fact, it is probably the best 'selfie' you could ever have! Astrology can not only tell you who you are, but also how best to care for that self and your own specific needs and desires as revealed by your birth-chart.

Self-care is simply time to look after yourself – to restore, inspirit and refresh and love your unique self. But it's also about understanding, accepting and being aware of your own traits – both the good and not so good – so that you can then say, 'It's ok to be me, and my intention is to become the best of myself'. In fact, by looking up to the stars and seeing how they reflect us down here on Earth, we can deepen our connection to the Universe for the good of all, too. Understanding that caring about ourselves is not selfish creates an awesome sense of self-acceptance and awareness.

So how does each of us honour the individual 'me' and find the right kind of rituals and practices to suit our personalities? Astrology sorts us out into the zodiac – an imaginary belt encircling the Earth divided into twelve sun signs; so, for example, what one sign finds relaxing, another may find a hassle or stressful. When it comes to physical fitness, adventurous Arians thrive on aerobic work, while soulful Pisceans feel nurtured by yoga. Financial reward or status would inspire the ambitious Capricorn mind, while theatrical Leos need to indulge their joy of being centre stage.

By knowing which sun sign you are and its associated characteristics, you will discover the right self-care routines and practices to suit you. And this unique and empowering book is here to help – with all the rituals and practices in these pages specifically suited to your sun-sign personality for nurturing and vitalising your mind, body and spirit.

However, self-care is not an excuse to be lazy and avoid the goings on in the rest of the world. Self-care is about taking responsibility for our choices and understanding our unique essence, so that we can engage with all aspects of ourselves and the way we interact with the world.

IN A NUTSHELL

Pisces is a bit of a chameleon, a sign who seems to embody the shadows and light of all the other zodiac signs. Romantic and highly imaginative, Pisceans' dreamy nature casts a spell of serenity on those around them. The two fish swimming away from one another symbolise the dual nature of this Mutable sign: one who heads towards the calm waters of poetry in motion, and the other who flounders in a sea of everyone else's identities. By both caring for your intuitive self and learning a little healthy selfishness, you will discover a true sense of who you are, to find the joy and happiness you truly deserve. This book will show you how to care for all of you, so you can follow the pathway to being your authentic self..

Sun-Sign Astrology

Also known as your star sign or zodiac sign, your sun sign encompasses the following:

* Your solar identity, or sense of self
* What really matters to you
* Your future intentions
* Your sense of purpose
* Various qualities that manifest through your actions, goals, desires and the personal sense of being 'you'
* Your sense of being 'centred' – whether 'self-centred' (too much ego) or 'self-conscious' (too little ego); in other words, how you perceive who you are as an individual

In fact, the sun tells you how you can 'shine' best to become who you really are.

ASTROLOGY FACTS

The zodiac or sun signs are twelve 30-degree segments that create an imaginary belt around the Earth. The zodiac belt is also known as the ecliptic, which is the apparent path of the sun as it travels round the Earth during the year.

The sun or zodiac signs are further divided into four elements (Fire, Earth, Air and Water, denoting a certain energy ruling each sign), plus three modalities (qualities associated with how we inter-act with the world; these are known as Cardinal, Fixed and Mutable). So as a Piscean, for example, you are a 'Mutable Water' sign.

* Fire signs: Aries, Leo, Sagittarius
  They are: extrovert, passionate, assertive

* Earth signs: Taurus, Virgo, Capricorn
  They are: practical, materialistic, sensual

* Air signs: Gemini, Libra, Aquarius
  They are: communicative, innovative, inquisitive

* Water signs: Cancer, Scorpio, Pisces
  They are: emotional, intuitive, understanding

The modalities are based on their seasonal resonance according to the northern hemisphere.

Cardinal signs instigate and initiate ideas and projects.
They are: Aries, Cancer, Libra and Capricorn

Fixed signs resolutely build and shape ideas.
They are: Taurus, Leo, Scorpio and Aquarius

Mutable signs generate creative change and adapt ideas to reach a conclusion.

They are: Gemini, Virgo, Sagittarius and Pisces

Planetary rulers

Each zodiac sign is assigned a planet, which highlights the qualities of that sign:

Aries is ruled by Mars (fearless)
Taurus is ruled by Venus (indulgent)
Gemini is ruled by Mercury (magical)
Cancer is ruled by the moon (instinctive)
Leo is ruled by the sun (empowering)
Virgo is ruled by Mercury (informative)
Libra is ruled by Venus (compassionate)
Scorpio is ruled by Pluto (passionate)
Sagittarius is ruled by Jupiter (adventurous)
Capricorn is ruled by Saturn (disciplined)
Aquarius is ruled by Uranus (innovative)
Pisces is ruled by Neptune (imaginative)

Opposite Signs

Signs oppose one another across the zodiac (i.e. those that are 180 degrees away from each other) – for example, Pisces opposes Virgo and Taurus opposes Scorpio. We often find ourselves mysteriously attracted to our opposite signs in romantic relationships, and while the signs' traits appear to clash in this 'polarity', the essence of each is contained in the other (note, they have the same modality). Gaining insight into the characteristics of your opposite sign (which are, essentially, inherent in you) can deepen your understanding of the energetic interplay of the horoscope.

On The Cusp

Some of us are born 'on the cusp' of two signs – in other words, the day or time when the sun moved from one zodiac sign to another. If you were born at the end or beginning of the dates usually given in horoscope pages (the sun's move through one sign usually lasts approximately four weeks), you can check which sign you are by contacting a reputable astrologer (or astrology site) (see Resources, p. 115) who will calculate it exactly for you. For example, 23 August is the standardised changeover day for the sun to move into Virgo and out of Leo. But every year, the time and even sometimes the day the sun changes sign can differ. So, say you were born on 23 August at five in the morning and the sun didn't move into Virgo until five in the afternoon on that day, you would be a Leo, not a Virgo.

How To Use This Book

The book is divided into three parts, each guiding you in applying self-care to different areas of your life:

* Part One: your mind and feelings
* Part Two: your body
* Part Three: your soul

Caring about the mind using rituals or ideas tailored to your sign shows you ways to unlock stress, restore focus or widen your perception. Applying the practices in Part One will connect you to your feelings and help you to acknowledge and become aware of why your emotions are as they are and how to deal with them. This sort of emotional self-care will set you up to deal with your relationships better, enhance all forms of communication and ensure you know exactly how to ask for what you want or need, and be true to your deepest desires.

A WORD ON CHAKRAS

Eastern spiritual traditions maintain that universal energy, known as 'prana' in India and 'chi' in Chinese philosophy, flows through the body, linked by seven subtle energy centres known as chakras (Sanskrit for 'wheel'). These energies are believed to revolve or spiral around and through our bodies, vibrating at different frequencies (corresponding to seven colours of the light spectrum) in an upward, vertical direction. Specific crystals are placed on the chakras to heal, harmonise, stimulate or subdue the chakras if imbalance is found.

The seven chakras are:
* The base or root (found at the base of the spine)
* The sacral (mid-belly)
* The solar plexus (between belly and chest)
* The heart (centre of chest)
* The throat (throat)
* The third eye (between the eyebrows)
* The crown (top of the head)

On p. 91 we will look in more detail at how Pisceans can work with chakras for self-care.

Fitness and caring for the body are different for all of us, too. While Pisces benefits from meditation or reflexology, Sagittarius prefers to go for a run, and Gemini a daily quick stretch or yoga. Delve into Part Two whenever you're in need of physical restoration or a sensual makeover tailored to your sign.

Spiritual self-care opens you to your sacred self or soul. Which is why Part Three looks at how you can nurture your soul according to your astrological sun sign. It shows you how to connect to and care for your spirituality in simple ways, such as being at one with Nature or just enjoying the world around you. It will show you how to be more positive about who you are and honour your connection to the Universe. In fact, all the rituals and practices in this section will bring you joyful relating, harmonious living and a true sense of happiness.

The Key

Remember, your birth-chart or horoscope is like the key to a treasure chest containing the most precious jewels that make you you. Learn about them, and care for them well. Use this book to polish, nurture, respect and give value to the beautiful gemstones of who you are, and, in doing so, bring your potential to life. It's your right to be true to who you are, just by virtue of being born on this planet, and therefore being a child of Mother Earth and the cosmos.

Care for you, and you care for the Universe.

PISCES
WORDS OF WISDOM

As you embark on your self-care journey, it's important to look at the lunar cycles and specific astrological moments throughout the year. At those times (and, indeed, at any time you choose), the words of Pisces wisdom below will be invaluable, empowering you with positive energy. Taking a few mindful moments at each of the four major phases of every lunar cycle and at the two important astrological moments in your solar year (see Glossary, p. 117) will affirm and enhance your positive attitude towards caring about your-self and the world.

NEW CRESCENT MOON – to care for yourself:

'I connect to my soulful way of perceiving life.'

'I believe that my dreams will come true if I take time to focus.'

'I know that I love and am loved.'

FULL MOON – for sealing your intention to care for your feeling world:

'I see that my soul is one among many, and we are all unique in that, yet at the same time we are all the same, for we share the soul of the Universe.'

'Trusting my intuition will bring me the happiness I seek.'

'I know what I want, so I must care about sticking to my true intention.'

WANING MOON – for letting go, and letting things be:

'I must stop being so sensitive to others and create my own boundaries.'

'No longer will I get lost in love but instead get found by loving myself.'

'Let my feelings flow, but let me not sacrifice my true intentions.'

DARK OF THE MOON – to acknowledge your 'shadow' side:

'Forgiveness leads to healing, not martyrdom.'

'Giving everything away of myself won't let me find myself.'

'Happiness is within reach if I stop running from the truth.'

SOLAR RETURN SALUTATION – welcoming your new solar year to be true to who you are:

Affirm on your birthday: 'I will learn to make use of my creative and imaginative powers and discover my true vocation in life.'

SUN IN OPPOSITION – learn to be open to the opposite perspective that lies within you:

Repeat when the sun is in Virgo: 'My opposite sign is Virgo, a sign of discrimination and emotional detachment. These attributes are in my birth-chart, too, so I must learn to organise my life rather than feel it is a cross to bear. Then I will feel more relaxed in myself and find time for all those dreams and visions to be be realised.'

The Pisces Personality

$$\mathord{\text{♓}}$$

I love you not only for what you are,
but for what I am when I am with you.
Elizabeth Barrett Browning, English poet

Characteristics: Mysterious, romantic, subtle, elusive, changeable, gullible, intuitive, psychic, receptive, escapist, artistic, self-sacrificing, compassionate, unfocused, self-doubting, sentimental, dreamy, unreliable, indecisive, unpredictable, imaginative

Symbol: two Fish
The symbol of the constellation Pisces is represented by two Fish joined by a golden thread, yet swimming in opposite directions. Greek myth tells of how, while fleeing from the monster Typhon, Aphrodite and her son Eros saved themselves by shape-shifting into two fish, then heading in different directions to fool the monster.

Planetary ruler: Neptune (traditionally Jupiter)
This dark, icy giant is not only the planet furthest
from the sun (apart from the dwarf planet Pluto,
which is not a true planet), but also the windiest in the
solar system. Clouds of frozen methane are whipped
across it by supersonic winds at speeds of more than
1,200 miles per hour. The planet's rich sea-blue colour
is thought to be due to the gases of the atmosphere.

Astrological Neptune: In the birth-chart, Neptune
describes our dreams, fantasies, longings,
compassion and ideals of love. Neptune's realm also
relates to deception, sacrifice, glamourisation and
seduction, not forgetting loss and redemption.

Element: Water
Like Scorpio and Cancer, Pisces is a 'feeling' sign. In
other words, what the Water signs feel is what is real
to them. They are subjective and soulful, and
decisions are made based on 'gut' instinct and
emotional motivation. Water signs have an intuitive
understanding of how to flow with the undercurrents
and moods of others. Pisces floats on this tide of
feeling to take them away from harsh reality.

Modality: Mutable
Flexible, creative, spontaneous, quick-thinking,
changeable, restless. As with the other Mutable

signs, Gemini, Sagittarius and Virgo, Pisces marks the changeover from one season to another, in this case from winter to spring.

Body: Feet, immune system, pineal gland

Crystal: Amethyst

Sun-sign profile: As the last sign of the zodiac, Pisces is the most complex. In astrology, it is believed that each sun- sign carries a little of the qualities of the previous signs within its essence. So, for example, Aries, as the first, is considered the most single-minded, egocentric, selfish and the least complex. The second sign, Taurus, carries the selfishness of Aries, yet finds a practical application for that self and so on. As the last sign, Pisces embodies all the psychic energies of the previous eleven – their desires, their dreams, their longings and their needs. In fact, this connection to the collective unconscious enables the Fish to quickly empathise with other people, often giving up their own desires to make them feel happy. But like the sign of two fish swimming in opposite directions, Pisces is a paradox: one side submerges itself in the sea of escapism when 'reality' is too much for their sensitive soul to bear; the other brings to light its imaginative world through art, poetry, music, mystical beliefs or human love.

The idealistic and changeable Fish also has a problem with boundaries, and often finds it easier to identify with whoever they are with because they haven't yet found their own sense of authenticity.

Known for their altruistic, non-judgmental outlook on life, Pisceans find it hard to make a choice. There are so many possibilities, so many different truths – how can you choose one over another? Everything is 'relative' to Pisces, and so it's hardly surprising to learn that one of the greatest developments in history, the theory of relativity, was by Albert Einstein – a Piscean. Likewise, if a Piscean can put those dreams to some use, then the Fish starts to swim with the tide, instead of against it.

Your best-kept secret: Knowing there is something divine within you

What gives you meaning and purpose in life? Caring for and healing others, dreams that can be fulfilled one day, expressing universal truths through your creativity

What makes you feel good to be you? Peaceful surroundings, a low-pressure environment, space to do your own thing, being at one with Nature

What or who do you identify with? Artists, musicians, dreamers, saints, actors, poets, fictional characters, healers, mystics, gurus, carers, victims, saviours, animals, charities

What stresses you out? Direct confrontation, making decisions, harsh reality, egotists, people who don't care about animals, expectations of others, commitments, having to be punctual

What relaxes you? Weepy films, music, art, candlelit dinners, acting, being creative, being in the company of animals or Nature

What challenges you? Learning a healthy selfishness, putting your own needs first, goal setting, being emotionally detached from others

What Does Self-Care Mean For Pisces?

Rather like the other Mutable signs, Gemini, Sagittarius and Virgo, Pisces isn't awfully good at sticking to routines, being slotted into a time frame or making a regular commitment. In fact, no routine is the only way for Pisces to enjoy some self-care – just whenever the moment feels right, or when, say, they intuitively know they need to go for a walk in the countryside, have a day's detox or roll out the yoga mat. The less Pisces is told to do something, the more likely they are to do it, but always in their own time and in their own way.

When it comes to the notion of self-care generally, horror of horrors that the Fish must take care of themselves first and others second. Surely that's egotistic and completely at odds with their innate gift for looking after everyone else? But unless you truly believe in caring for you, and how you evolve and grow to become the best of yourself, then you can't actually help anyone else.

So it's time to turn the spotlight on to you. This book will enable you to boost your self-worth, care for your Pisces soul and nurture your innate compassion without giving away too much of your emotional self. By spending more time looking after yourself, you will change your world for the better and realise you have every right to be the kind, gentle and imaginative Pisces you are.

Self-Care Focus

Cultivate your self-care garden around your own needs, not those of others. Deal with life's stresses by simply restoring your deep awareness of what is healthy and what does you good – find time to be alone, to chill out, to relax and to work in a pressure-free environment. Pisces rules the feet, so to help you stay grounded, go walking, dancing or even garden-ing to feel a physical connection to the Earth itself. Then enjoy your creative imagination and express it in the tangible world. By helping yourself first, you can become the perfect role model for others.

Your powerful, intuitive mind and the way you can tap into the collective unconscious are wonderful gifts for your creative potential. You don't have to believe in the gods, but magic, mysticism and esoteric thinking will bring you a deeper connection to your sacred self and provide a layer of protection against the 'real' world.

This book will delight you with the kind of care that brings out the best of you, so you can truly find happiness and joy in life, while realising that hidden potential, so that you can take this exciting journey to who you are becoming.

PART ONE

Caring For Your Mind And Feelings

I never made one of my discoveries
through the process of rational thinking.

Albert Einstein

This section will inspire you to delight in your thoughts, express your ideas and take pleasure in your feelings. Once you get that deep sense of awareness of who you are and what you need, not only will it feel good to be alive, but you will be even more content to be yourself. The rituals and practices here will boost your self-esteem, motivate you to lead a more serene existence and enhance all forms of relationships with others. The most important relationship of all, with yourself, will be nurtured in the best possible way according to your sun sign.

What you see is not what you get with a Piscean, who sees life from many different perspectives and often avoids speaking the truth, simply because they don't know what the truth is. After all, there are so many possibilities. Pisces has an intuitive understanding of human nature and knows that what is right to one person may be wrong to another. There are grey areas in life – nothing is black and white – and that means the Fish can't be classified either. If you try to put Pisceans into a category (including the fact that they're Pisceans), they'll usually quietly disappear through the nearest exit.

Neptune, the planet of spiritual longing, escapism, self-sacrifice and redemption, rules Pisces. So it's hardly surprising that the Fish has a problem with reality and tends to fall back on their 'now-you-see-me-now-you-don't' attitude. And that includes the reality of who they are and what they really think. How can they define themselves when they are constantly slipping into different roles, depending on who they are with? The Fish finds it easy to listen to their intuition, but less so to express their feelings and thoughts. So the practices in this section will encourage you to care about developing a positive mindset, while helping you to express your needs and desires, and be unafraid of having a mind of your own.

MOTIVATION CHARM

✳

Pisces knows only too well how hard it is to get motivated for any self-care programme when there are so many things that need to be done at work, around the house, helping others out and so on. In fact, why not just put it all off, anyway? But it's this distinct lack of focus and attention that means you miss out on giving love to the most important person in your world: you.

Here's how to conjure up the spirit of motivation and get started on cultivating your 'self-care garden'. This ritual is best performed on a waxing-moon evening to maximise the lunar energy to fulfil your intention.

You will need:
* A very small plant pot (or, if you have an outside space, a dedicated spot in which to plant your motivation charm)
* A handful of basil leaves (for focus)
* A handful of sage leaves (for understanding)
* A handful of lavender flowers (for self-love)
* 5 small pieces of red carnelian (for motivation)
* A pearl

1. Fill your little pot or hole first with the basil leaves, then a layer of sage, then a layer of lavender.

2. Finally, place the red carnelian on top.

3. Hold the pearl between your hands, close to your belly, and say the following: 'This pearl will bring me the focus and strength to love myself first and care for that loving, and not be led astray or distracted by others'.

4. Kiss the pearl, then place it in the middle of your petition to the Universe.

5. If you have chosen an outside space for this, cover the offering with a sprinkling of pebbles or stones to mark the spot; if it's in an indoor pot, place it near a window to draw down the lunar and solar energy.

By the full moon, you will feel ready to get any self-care programme working. And whenever you feel lacking in motivation, just return to your offering and hold the pearl (removing the stones first if outdoors).

CULTIVATING SELF-BELIEF

♡

The next problem with Pisces self-care is having enough self-belief to keep you focused and enthusiastic about being special. One of the biggest Pisces dilemmas is how can you believe in yourself, if you don't really know what there is about you to believe in?

Belief is everything – it shapes our lives, dreams and desires. Believing in the magic of yourself is the key to a positive, defined and grounded you. So here's a ritual to put self-belief into focus, and really feel you have your own unique identity; plus, it will help you to feel grounded in the here and now.

You will need:
* 2 red candles
* A piece of malachite
* A piece of onyx
* A piece of turquoise
* A clear quartz crystal
* A piece of paper and a pen

1. Light the candles.

2. Set the crystals out in a row.

3. To invoke your own sense of being grounded, write the following words on your piece of paper (in a row, in the same order): 'Trust', 'Integrity', 'Belief', 'Self'.

4. Next, place each crystal on its corresponding word: so malachite on 'Trust', onyx on 'Integrity', turquoise on 'Belief' and the quartz on 'Self'.

5. Now change the order of the crystals, randomly moving them around, so the row is no longer the same. The words are still there – they haven't changed; only the crystals have moved. And the crystals themselves haven't changed intrinsically either, only their positions. It's all relative, isn't it? Yet trust, integrity, belief and self remain fixed within you, even if everything on the outside moves, changes or evolves.

6. Finish by saying this affirmation to invoke self-belief by the bucketload:

As I believe in me, I grow and learn.
Integrity allows me to find my turn.
As I accept others, I shape my trust
To love others less and myself the best.
So believing in me will ground and define me,
My identity shaped as it should be.

Cultivating an awareness of how life can move around you while your inner core remains stable will enable you to develop your own ego strength. Repeat this ritual whenever you feel a sense of disconnection from your self to restore you and remind you that being true to your individuality will give you purpose and strength of character.

....

SELF-LOVE SANCTUARY

⭐

You may well dedicate yourself to caring for others – it's natural for Pisceans to give their hearts away – but learning a healthy selfishness (rather than selflessness) means you can start putting your own needs first and honour your astrological purpose, which is to fulfil your dreams and express your imaginative soul to the world.

With this in mind, why not create this sanctuary dedicated to you and you alone? Find a space in your home that you can call your own; it doesn't have to be anything grand – just a corner of a table, a low footstool or a designated area of the floor will do.

You will need:

* A photo of yourself (the most important ingredient)
* An item with positive associations – a symbol of things that bring you joy
* An image of flowers or herbs
* A favourite crystal
* A votive candle

1. Arrange the above items as you like. As you place them, appreciate what they mean to you. You may want to decorate your sanctuary with fresh flowers, shells, images of the sea or other symbols that you adore, but most of all build this space with love for yourself, dedicated to who you are.

2. Once your sanctuary is created, light your candle, find stillness and ground yourself into this place by saying the following affirmations:

> I appreciate all my skills and talents and will share them wisely.
>
> I give value to my kindness and caring nature, and therefore offer kindness and care to myself.
>
> I respect my need to look after me first, and others second.
>
> I honour my Pisces self, and will learn to no longer be *selfless*, but carve an identity for *myself*.

Visit your sanctuary at least once a week, light your candle, repeat the above affirmations, admire your collection and add to it as often as you like, to show a growing commitment to loving yourself.

....

LUNAR PLANTING

✳

Any Piscean knows that the moon has a powerful influence on their mind and feelings. When it is full, for example, the Fish often feels overcome by other people's problems; at the dark of the new moon, they are more psychic and with the new crescent moon, they are more creative. But even though your creativity often gets lost among the emotional tides of the lunar cycle, with this practice the moon is going to be your best friend and guide.

Planting seeds according to the cycles of the moon is a well-known tradition in gardening folklore, and it can also be used as a symbolic intention to evolve, grow and unleash your true potential on to the world, whether as the mystic wise woman or the artistic genius.

This ritual asks you to symbolically plant the following items during one lunar cycle and then harvest your innate gifts. Even if you don't know what these are yet, this practice will give you an awareness of that potential.

You will need:

* A candle
* A small box with a lid, a pouch or any container of your choice

* A few handfuls of sunflower seeds
* An acorn
* A gold-coloured coin
* A piece of rose quartz
* A piece of black tourmaline or onyx
* Frankincense essential oil

Part one:
1. Begin your lunar ritual during the evening of the new crescent moon, by lighting your candle.
2. Fill your box with the sunflower seeds.
3. 'Plant' the acorn into the seeds. As you do so, say: 'With this acorn, I will give growth to my talents'.
4. Focus on your desire for creative growth, and as you blow out the candle thank the Universe for its help.

Part two:
1. On the evening of a waxing moon (about a week later), light your candle again.
2. Open your box and 'plant' the coin. Say, 'With this golden coin, I plant my creativity and see it flourish'.

Part three:
1. On the evening of the full moon, relight your candle.
2. Now 'plant' your rose quartz and say, 'With rose quartz, I plant loving energy to my creative self, and do

not fear my feelings, but work with them for a bountiful harvest'.

Part four:
1. On the evening of a waning moon (about a week later), relight your candle.
2. 'Plant' the black tourmaline or onyx and say, 'I plant this crystal to protect myself from negativity and banish all worries'.

Part five:
1. On the evening of the dark of the new moon, relight your candle.
2. 'Plant' the frankincense oil by dropping one or two drops on to the contents of your box, and say: 'With frankincense, I will grow the shoots of creativity, nurture my gifts of imagination, whether mystical or artistic, and manifest my talents'.

By the end of the next lunar cycle, you will know what it is you need to manifest in the world, and you will find your creativity flourishes.

....

BE YOURSELF

♡

In Celtic myth, Cerridwen was the shape-shifting goddess of magic, inspiration and poetry, transforming herself into any being or creature she desired. Similarly, Pisceans have a habit of shaping their identity into a mirror image of the one they're with, and then end up losing all sense of who they are.

Use this goddess ritual to promote your own sense of authenticity, and to liberate yourself from other people's influences.

Perform this practice during a waning-moon phase.

You will need:
* A pink tea light
* A handful of lavender flowers
* A bowl of spring water
* A mirror
* A piece of amethyst

1. Light your candle.

2. Scatter the lavender flowers over the surface of the water.

3. Look into the mirror and focus on your image. For a few moments, consider who you really are and who you want to be – an imaginative, intuitive, mystical soul? A poet? A caring, loving person? A family- and nature-loving carer?

4. Now put the amethyst into the bowl and stir your finger gently around three times in an anticlockwise direction, as you say: 'With this amethyst and Cerridwen's help I will find my true self among others. I will no longer let others influence me.'

5. Take the amethyst out of the water and hold it to the middle of your forehead, as you gaze into the mirror again, visualising your individuality growing as real and as solid as the crystal.

6. Leave the petition to Cerridwen overnight and keep the crystal in a safe place.

Whenever you feel lost in the stormy sea of other people's energies, take the crystal and hold it to your forehead to boost your ego and find your authentic inner strength.

THE NEREID IN YOU

One of the planet Neptune's moons is named after the sea nymphs of Greek mythology, the Nereids. The Nereids were kind to lost ships and to sailors, calming the sea after Poseidon's raging storms, and they told the mysteries of the gods to enlighten heroic mortals such as Aeneas. However, another group of sea nymphs were the terrifying Sirens, who sang beautiful love songs to lure sailors to follow them down into the ocean – and drown them. This could serve as an analogy for the Pisces dilemma: the Nereid in you who can access the depths of the imagination and bring it to light in the tangible world; and the Siren in you who drowns her talents in a sea of escapism.

Now it's time to care for the Nereid in you and let that imagination come to life.

You will need:

* Your journal or just a very large piece of paper to create a Pisces masterpiece

1. Write either or both of the following affirmations boldly across your paper: 'I need to open myself to my imagination' and/or, 'I honour and express my sacred self through my talents'.

2. You can also illustrate the affirmations, adding images, leaves, flowers or photos or create a collage that showcases these feelings and inspirations.

This can be a work in progress, added to when you 'feel' inspired. Or you can just turn to it, gaze at it and feel uplifted by your artwork. It doesn't matter if you never finish it; it doesn't matter if you change it. What matters is that you're at last caring for the Nereid – in other words, that innate imaginative force in you – and bringing it into the light of day.

VISUALISATION FOR INTUITION

✳

Pisceans are known to be highly intuitive, yet sometimes they are led astray by the facts and figures, and doing what is 'right', rather than following their instincts. Here's a way to restore and develop that kind of psychic mind:

1. Sit somewhere alone, where you can ensure a deeper level of receptivity, relax and breathe quietly.

2. Close your eyes and visualise yourself walking down a long road.

3. You come across a cave and decide to stop there for a while.

4. In the cave, you sit down on a golden throne to rest. A shaft of pure white light beams down on you through a crevice in the roof of the cave. You feel the power of this spiritual energy filling your body, flowing through every part of you, from your head down to your toes.

5. Now, with your psychic energy topped up, you walk out of the cave and carry on down the road.

6. You approach a corner. What is around the corner? Intuitively, you know. At this moment, in your imagination, whatever comes into your head, imagine it being around the corner. (You might, for example, imagine you meet a clown, a man with a dog, a lion or a beautiful stranger – whatever you like.)

7. Now in your visualisation, meet the entity you have imagined. Say 'Hello', offer them your best wishes and continue on your way.

8. Come out of your visualisation and relax back to normal.

For the next few days, remind yourself to follow your intuition. So for example, every time you open a door, walk around a street corner or are about to pick up the phone, let your intuition 'speak' to you in its own way. You may not always be right, but with practice, your intuitive sense can become your best one.

BOUNDARIES AND LIMITS

♡

Pisceans find the necessities of everyday life – such as money, housework and, most of all (although they try not to admit it), other people's demands – draining on their sensitive psyches. Their ability to escape responsibility by running off with the metaphorical fairies is all very well, but what's also needed is an awareness of their limits and how to say 'No', nicely.

Take a few quiet minutes on a waxing-moon evening to try this ritual, and you'll be surprised at how it will help you to appreciate when to say, 'No' or, 'Hang on – I need to reflect before I make a commitment' or even simply, 'I'm sorry. I just can't help right now.'

You will need:
* 4 pieces of smoky quartz (or brown/black pebbles)
* A length of string, ribbon or twine (about 30–38cm or 12–15 inches)
* A tea light

1. Place the four stones around the tea light to form the corners of a square.

2. Wind the ribbon around the outside of the square to create a boundary all the way around.

3. Light the candle and say, 'I see my light shining bright and know my limits'.

4. Touch each of the stones in turn and say, 'I have boundaries as solid as these stones'.

5. Next, touch the ribbon and say, 'With this ribbon, I defend myself from the feelings of others'.

6. Pick up the ribbon and wind it around your wrist as you say, 'I am no longer a sponge absorbing emotions, but a stronghold of self-reliance'.

Keep the ribbon and stones in a safe place, so you can repeat the charm any time you need to boost your sense of boundaries. You have created an imaginary, yet magical moat to keep yourself safe – respect it, and you respect yourself.

DECISION MAKING

One of the biggest stress triggers for Pisceans is making decisions. Frankly, how can you choose one thing over another?

Here's how to make a decision and still be stress-free.

You will need:
* 2 pieces of paper and a pen
* 2 pieces of clear quartz crystal (about the same size)
* A large paper bag

1. Reflect on making your decision for a minute or so.

2. Write down on each piece of paper the two possibilities: 'I am going to do X' and 'I am going to do Y'.

3. Fold a piece of paper around each crystal and put them into the bag.

4. Shake the bag gently, so you don't know which crystal is which.

5. Leave the bag on a table, go for a walk and enjoy a change of scenery to clear your mind.

6. When you get home, put your hand straight into the bag and pull out the first paper-wrapped crystal you touch.

7. Unfold the paper and review your 'choice'. You will intuitively realise that this is the right one for this moment in time.

Keep the chosen crystal with you to remind you that if you stick to your choice, you won't regret it.

Relationships

The gregarious Fish depends on their social and family network to give them the love it is so hard for them to find in themselves. It's one thing being the life and soul of the party, but the Fish forgets that love comes from within and not just from without. In fact, Pisceans often sacrifice their own goals and needs to ensure everyone else is happy, and then feel short-changed. The way to bring joy to yourself, as well as others is, yes, to care for the world, but to care for the gentle, loving soul that you are, too.

In love, Pisces is one of the most romantic and charismatic of signs. Merging with whoever they fall for, they intuitively know how to seduce their admirer. In fact, the Fish will do anything for their lover – give up their job, romanticise about the future, talk about the same goals and even clean their car to win a few 'practical' gold stars. We've seen how the Fish has a problem with boundaries, which is why they are easy targets for the more calculating Romeos, looking for anything other than commitment. Pisceans can also get lost further down the relationship commitment line through not having known what they truly needed or wanted to begin with.

Traditional relationships may sound romantic on paper, but when the reality of daily routines sets in, and the car really does need cleaning every week, the Fish may run for the hills. Sensual, mystical, intuitive and deeply loving, they need to be needed, and the changeable, idealistic and dependent Pisces will find happiness in a long-term love relationship as long as they also have space to dream awhile.

WELCOMING LOVE

✳

Pisces may love people, but if you're trying to please everyone all the time, and not much pleasing yourself, you're losing out on the greatest relationship of all – with you. To remind you that love is unconditional and that you don't have to be someone you're not, this ritual – performed every new crescent moon – will get others to love you for being the 'real' you; but also, *you* can begin to love the real you better, too.

You will need:
* A mirror
* A pin or needle
* 3 white candles

1. Sit comfortably before the mirror.

2. Using the pin or needle, carve along the length of each candle, as follows: on the first, 'I welcome love'; on the second, 'It is mine'; and on the third, 'To give and take'.

3. Now light the candles and focus on each of the flames for a few moments, in turn.

4. Next, gaze at your reflection in the mirror and say, 'I welcome love – it is mine to give and take'.

5. Let the candles burn down until all, or at least some, of the carved letters have melted.

As a Piscean, you will know intuitively when to blow out the flames and realise that your heart is now open to the right kind of love that soothes, heals and cares for your gentle soul.

. . . .

WISHING PEARLS

✳

The ancient gem of the sea, the pearl has many myths and legends attached to it, but it is symbolic of loyalty, generosity and fidelity. In Greek mythology, it was believed that pearls were the tears of the gods of the sea, while in Hindu mythology they were dew drops that fell from the moon into the ocean. In Greek folklore, a pearl was often tossed into the sea when making a wish for new romance.

Changeable and restless, the Fish sometimes runs away from their romantic dreams when people don't live up to their ideal of what love is. This manifests as a sort of soft martyrdom when chatting to pals: 'They didn't really understand me', 'We weren't on the same wavelength', 'Never mind – plenty more fish in the sea'.

This wishing ritual cuts through illusions and ideals to see the truth of love and to attract the kind of lover or partner you truly long for – one who respects your mutable, restless nature and is respectful of you being you.

You will need:

* 2 white candles
* 2 pearls
* Ylang-ylang essential oil

1. On the evening of a full moon, light the two candles.

2. Place a pearl in front of each candle.

3. Anoint each pearl with a drop of the essential oil.

4. Now think carefully about your wish. It can be as simple as 'I wish to meet my soulmate', or more detailed – 'I'm looking for someone who fulfils all my expectations, which are . . .' Whatever your wish is, you must mean it and *believe* that it will come true. (You might want to do the exercise on p. 45 first, if you need to restore self-belief.)

5. Pick up the pearls in turn and say your wish aloud each time.

6. Blow out the candles after, say, five minutes (or when you intuitively know the moment is right) and leave your petition overnight.

7. In the morning, put the pearls in your handbag or pocket.

By the next full moon, you will encounter the person you have wished for.

FOR LONG-TERM HARMONY

✱

When lovers lock a padlock to a bridge railing and throw the key in the river, they are showing their fidelity. Similarly, the knotted votive in this charm will ensure you are tied in a perfect love knot and that the Piscean need for peace and harmony is locked into the relationship for ever.

You will need:

* 1 white candle
* 1 red candle
* 1 red ribbon
* 1 white ribbon

1. Carve your name on one candle and your partner's name on the other.

2. Tie the red ribbon in a knot at the base of the white candle, then wind it around and around, leaving about 5cm (2 inches) free at the end.

3. Do the same with the white ribbon around the red candle, again leaving a little free at the end.

4. Now tie the two ribbons together into a knot and light the candles.

5. Let the flames flicker (taking care that the knot is tied off well below the flames) and say the following affirmation: 'With this knot, our love for one another will always be strong and true. Our love is bound and tied here, and my Pisces heart is nurtured by my intention.'

6. Focus on your intention for a few minutes, then blow out the candles to seal your love-knot petition.

Keep the candles tied together and store in a safe place, both as a keepsake and symbolic empowerment of the knot you have tied in love.

PART TWO
Caring For Your Body

The body is the instrument
of our hold on the world.

Simone de Beauvoir, French
philosopher and writer

Here, you will discover alternative ways to look after and nurture your body, not just as a physical presence, but its connection to mind and spirit, too. This section gives you a wide range of ideas, from using sun-sign crystals to protect your physical and psychic self to fitness, diet and beauty tips. There are specific chakra practices and yoga poses especially suited to your sun sign, not forgetting bath-time rituals and calming practices to destress you and nurture holistic wellbeing.

Taking time to care for everyone else in the Pisces home, family or community means the Fish has little time left to pamper their physical self. As one of the more passive, independent signs of the zodiac, competitive team sports aren't really for you. And like the other Mutable signs, no routine is the best routine for Pisces, who hates being pinned down to time (rarely punctual) or feeling obliged to go to the same venue to keep fit (leads to boredom and daydreaming). When looking for a way to exercise, gentle stretching and breathing techniques such as yoga and Pilates, and fresh-air escapades such as walking, cycling or swimming will restore your energy levels.

Fitness and Movement

Pisces rules the feet, so anything that helps you to put your best foot forward will stimulate and improve your physical fitness. Also, any physical exercise involving music or water is food for the soul. Swimming is the obvious choice, but there is also ETM (exercise to music in water) or surfing, if you're a more adventurous Pisces. Having said that, while water sports are made for you, actually, you're more likely to be drifting downstream in a leisurely punt, beach-combing or living on a houseboat to get your much-needed water fix.

....

BEST FOOT FORWARD

♡

Dancing barefoot across a beach, through the surf or even on freshly mown grass will restore the Piscean metabolism, soothe your feet and ankles and support overall fitness. You don't have to have music – you can just sing a song, hum or imagine a tune or simply move rhythmically without a care in the world (other than caring for yourself).

Here's a way to incorporate this kind of free-form dance with a little more footwork for greater flexibility and suppleness of feet and legs.

1. Before you begin to dance, rest your leg on a bench or railing at about hip height.

2. Bend your ankle forwards and point the toes down, as if you were a ballerina, then flex your ankle back, until your toes are pointing up towards your knees. Repeat this stretch 10 times for each foot.

3. Stand up straight and rise on to your tiptoes for as long as is comfortable, then walk forwards on tiptoes for about 10 steps. Relax and repeat 3 more times.

4. Now, with your newly flexible ankles and toes, dance the light fantastic.

Enjoy the feel of the sand, water or land beneath your feet, and feel that sense of being grounded through your soles right up to the top of your head.

....

YOGA

♡

There's no fixed time or place for yoga, but if you can manage a few sessions of, say, twenty minutes a go to roll out that mat and enjoy the stillness within movement, you will benefit not only body, but soul too. Here's one pose you can perform whenever you have a spontaneous desire to feel energised, yet stress-free.

Child's pose

This is one of the simplest, yet most powerful of yoga poses. In this posture, your chakra energies will flow from your third-eye chakra down and around your body, awakening you to your inner life.

1. Kneel on your yoga mat (or soft ground). Separate your legs about hip-width apart and sit on your heels.

2. Exhale slowly as you lean forwards and fold the top half of your body over your legs.

3. Rest your forehead on the mat (be mindful that this is the location of the third-eye chakra, which will be stimulated even more and improve energy flow – see p. 91) and close your eyes.

4. Stretch your arms out in front of your body with palms resting on the mat and perhaps the fingers of both hands touching to create a circuit of energy.

5. While you are in this position, quietly observe your breath, as it fills your abdomen and right down each side of the ribcage. Bring your awareness to your pelvic area and notice how you feel opened with each breath.

6. Stay in this pose for about 2 or 3 minutes (don't fall asleep!), then gently return to sitting on your heels, before rising to a standing position.

7. Put your hands together in prayer pose in front of your chest; and, of course, give thanks to your practice: '*namaste*'.

Child's pose will help you to get in touch with the movement and flow of air within your core and calm and stabilise the often-fluctuating Piscean nervous system.

....

CHAIR PADDLING

♡

Even if you can sometimes get out and enjoy some Pisces-centred water exercises, there are times when you will be stuck at home or at your desk. This simple practice will stimulate your Pisces-ruled feet, tone your legs and give you that sense of splashing your feet in some tranquil lake or stream, bringing a sense of overall wellbeing.

1. Find a quiet place to sit comfortably and close your eyes.

2. Imagine you are sitting on the edge of a stream or lake and your feet are dangling in the cool water.

3. Begin to 'paddle' your legs up and down, left leg, right leg, left leg, right leg and so on, without touching the floor, keeping your toes pointed, as if you were splashing them in and out of the water.

4. Keep going to whatever rhythm suits you. You can even play music that reminds you of water or a beat that is the right tempo for you.

Do this for, say, five minutes to stretch and tone all leg and feet muscles and to awaken you to the watery flow within you.

Nutrition

Not exactly top of Pisces' to-do list is planning or even thinking about their next meal. In fact, the Fish can easily be led astray by all the good things in life, living in a romantic dream in which candlelit dinners, the best wines and gourmet restaurants are the key to fulfilling their desires. And before they know it, they have lost track of when they last ate anything and what it was.

Here are two ways to help you care about your nutrition without having to fuss about diets and nutritional values.

....

YOGHURT SMOOTHIE

One meal you can't afford to go without, and which won't take up much of your Pisces here-there-and-everywhere time, is good old breakfast. Start the day with this low-carb smoothie (replenishes the Pisces imbalance of nutrients), to tone and destress the body.

You will need:
* 1 cup unsweetened almond milk
* ½ cup plain Greek yoghurt
* 1 frozen banana
* 1 cup frozen mixed berries
* A sprinkling of chia seeds

1. Put all the ingredients into a blender. If you don't have a frozen banana, use a couple of ice cubes instead to thicken the mix.

2. Blend until well mixed, and serve straight away.

Make this a regular morning treat to fuel your fast Pisces metabolism, so you can get on with your busy activities for the rest of the day.

....

MOCK-TAIL TIME

✦✦
✦

Look, you know you love a drink (unless you are one of those self-sacrificing Pisceans, who go to extremes and give up everything that's bad for them and live like nuns). But without giving up or giving in, you can make this delicious, hydrating drink (Pisceans are prone to dehydration) and feel smug about balancing the excess now and again with a 'mock-tail'.

You will need:
* 1 scoop of electrolyte hydration powder (easily available from health-food sources, and full of electrolytes and minerals to keep you hydrated)
* A glass of sparkling water
* 2 fresh lemon slices
* 4 or 5 fresh raspberries
* A few mint leaves

1. Mix the powder into the water.

2. Drop in the lemon slices and fresh raspberries and sprinkle with the mint leaves.

Enjoy this refreshing, hydrating drink at any time of day.

Beauty

I once had a Piscean pal who spent more time in the bathroom than a Leo (the archetypal diva of pampering). When she appeared through the doorway looking, well, very much as she did when she went in (naturally beautiful), I began to wonder why she'd spent so much time in there. I asked, and she told me she was just dithering about which foundation, shampoo, facial, mask, hand cream to choose. It all took so much time, and in the end, she just decided to forget it.

Luckily, Pisceans have such a natural radiance – an inner glow radiating through them – that they don't, in fact, need many beauty products.

Pisceans do need to look after their feet, though, to keep them grounded. Foot massage, pedicure or even just soaking in an Epsom-salt bath are perfect ways to destress your feet.

Learn a new skill, such as reflexology, or treat yourself to a few sessions to give your whole body a revitalising experience and reveal any stress points. Below are just a few tips to help you do this, while enhancing that natural Pisces magic and inner beauty.

....

DIVINE FOOT MASSAGE

*

Pisceans need to help others, which means they are often out and about, rushing here, there and everywhere and frequently on their feet all day, too. This also drains a Fish's energy levels.

So why not attend to your feet and pamper your toes with this relaxing, soothing massage, restoring your spirit and vitality into the bargain. And if you happen to have one of those mechanical foot baths, so much the better to finish off your spa session.

You will need:
* A pink candle
* A piece of amethyst
* A cup of almond oil
* A small bowl
* 2 drops of jasmine essential oil
* 2 drops of rose essential oil
* 1 drop of lavender essential oil

1. Light the candle and place the amethyst beside it.

2. Pour the almond oil into the bowl, then drizzle in the other oils, gently stirring with your finger.

3. Place the amethyst in the bowl, ensuring it is well covered with oil.

4. Remove the crystal and use it as a pumice stone, working it all over your feet, following all the curves, lines, angles, bones, pads and in between your toes. If the oil starts to diminish, just pop the crystal back into the mixture and swirl it around.

5. Carry on doing this for about five minutes per foot. Once you have finished, either relax with a foot bath or gently wipe off any excess oil, wiggle your toes and tell them you love them, and they will ground and support you wherever you go.

The herbal energies of the essential oils in this practice will relieve any tension and stress, while improving circulation, stimulating muscles and keeping those toes in perfect shape.

WATER-NYMPH BATH TIME

✳

Here's a complete mermaid indulgence to complement the Fish's sensitive skin and connection to the ocean. In Irish tradition, a seaweed bath-time ritual is still used to replenish and vitalise skin, mind and soul. Sea kelp is purifying, detoxifying and exfoliating, and will pamper and restore a sense of the oceanic essence of the Piscean psyche.

You will need:

* ¼ cup of organic seaweed powder (you can get this from specialist suppliers online)
* 4 green tea lights
* 4 pieces of aquamarine
* A few drops of lavender essential oil

1. Run your bath, add the powder and stir in with your hand.

2. Light the four candles and place one at each corner of the bath.

3. Place the crystals alongside the four candles.

4. Add the lavender oil to the bath and sink into the water.

It won't be long until you feel like a water-nymph, floating gently on the ripples of the calm sea. You'll be relaxed and peaceful as you soak up the beneficial minerals. The aquamarine crystals will also destress and restore a sense of inner beauty.

CHAKRA BALANCE

The body's chakras are the epicentres of the life-force energy flowing through all things (see p. 22).

Pisces is associated mostly with the third-eye or brow chakra, located between the eyebrows, just above the bridge of the nose. This is the chakra of insight and intuition, of self-understanding and higher perception and wisdom. It is concerned with listening to our intuitive 'inner voice' and is related to the spiritual nature of life, questioning reality, dreams and psychic awareness, such as clairvoyance or telepathy.

When the third-eye chakra is in balance, you can access your higher self and become more aware of your spirituality. You feel 'in tune' with the universal energy, and everything feels as if it's 'meant to be'. You can see the truth of any matter and understand what people are really thinking or feeling, without influencing your own emotions.

When this chakra is underactive, you may be blind to the truth, passive and unassertive, afraid of doing what's right for you and indecisive. You may not trust your intuition and be glib about anything spiritual. To boost this chakra, wear or carry labradorite and amethyst (both represent divine empowerment and spiritual clarity). This will restore your intuitive and psychic nature, as well as giving you strong imaginative and visualisation powers.

If this chakra is overactive, you can't come down to Earth, living with your head in the clouds and being totally irrational. Grounding your ideas is impossible and you detach yourself totally from other people's opinions or feelings. Wearing lapis lazuli (representing strength of mind, wisdom and understanding) will subdue this chakra.

General Wellbeing

Self-care for your general wellbeing is, among other things, about looking after your environment and how you interact with it. As Pisces is a physically and emotionally sensitive sign, it is important to create a harmonious atmosphere around you. By surrounding yourself with positive energy in the home or on your person as you interact with the world, you'll be shielded from geopathic stress (see Glossary, p. 117) and negativity. Here are some ways to protect and bring harmony to the Piscean sense of wellbeing.

....

AMETHYST GRID

♡

Traditionally associated with the sign of Pisces, amethyst has been used since ancient times as a cure for alcoholism, but keeping it on your person is thought to be helpful in overcoming all forms of addiction. The stone of spiritual healing and enlightenment, amethyst is also often used by mystics, psychics, healers and religious leaders for its intuitive, transcendent and spiritually awakening properties. Its calming influence on the mind makes the wearer kind and gentle, too. It also promotes peace, love, courage, protection and happiness.

Here's the perfect Pisces crystal protection and healing grid. Use it in your home to safeguard you and your family, and to invoke good feelings within all who live there.

Create your grid in a dedicated space in the south corner of your home, in a place where you can leave it all year round (apart from when you get out the duster!).

You will need:
* A pink candle
* 5 pieces of amethyst
* 5 clear quartz crystals
* A handful of rose petals or lavender flowers
* Rose essential oil

1. Light the candle to invoke calming energy.

2. Place the five amethysts in an evenly spread circle.

3. Between each amethyst, place the clear quartz crystals.

4. In the centre of your grid, sprinkle the petals or flowers to form a centrepiece.

5. Drizzle a few drops of rose essential oil over the flowers to anoint the petition.

6. Now focus on the grid for a few moments and make an intention for your home to be protected and blessed, for the happiness and wellbeing of all who live there. (You could even write this down in your journal or on a piece of paper and keep it in a safe place.)

7. Blow out the candle.

Leave the grid in place to generate healing and loving energy in the home.

....

AURA PURIFIER

♡

When we go out into the world, it's inevitable that we pick up energies from the environment and from other people, and you, as a Piscean, are much more vulnerable than many to negativity from other people. So it's time to dust off all that psychic debris from your aura to help banish the negativity.

This simple ritual is best done during a waning-moon phase.

1. Stand in a sunny spot outside, facing east (preferably on a windy day).

2. Close your eyes, feeling yourself rooted to the ground.

3. Stretch your writing arm out in front of you, then open your eyes and slowly turn in an anticlockwise direction to the north. Stop for a few seconds while you say: 'Here, the north winds will blow away the dust from my aura'.

4. Turn to the west (arm still pointing out in front of you) and say, 'Here, the west winds will send me fresh energy to cleanse and care'.

5. Turn to the south and say, 'Here, the south winds will warm and restore my aura grace'.

6. Finally, turn to the east and say, 'Here, the east winds will purify my aura and clear all negativity'.

7. Feel yourself rooted to the Earth for a minute and imagine the winds embracing you and caring for you. Open your eyes to end the ritual.

Whenever you feel overwhelmed by other people's psychic energy, perform this ritual to restore and tidy up your energy field.

PART THREE

Caring For Your Soul

Get thee to a nunnery

William Shakespeare, English
playwright and poet

This final section offers you tailored, fun, easy and amazing ways to connect to and care for your sacred self. This, in turn, means you will begin to feel at one with the joyous energy of the Universe. You don't have to sign up to any religion or belief system (unless you want to) – just take some time to experience uplifting moments through your interaction with the spiritual aspects of the cosmos. Care for your sun sign's soul centre, and you care about the Universe, too.

Pisces has a longing for something otherworldly, mystical or transcendent, to leave the harsh reality of life behind and drift on the tide of the numinous. If you're not already involved in some kind of religion or spiritual belief, then create a sacred space or altar at home and do ritual magic work alone, perhaps by harnessing the power of crystals, Nature or involving yourself in neopagan spirituality. Read up about the great mystics like Hildegarde of Bingen and how she used Nature's magic for happiness and health. Learn to develop your psychic skills or divination powers; cast the runes, read the tarot, seek out sacred places or just enjoy the experience of the cosmic energy running through you.

Here are some practices to awaken you to your spiritual powers and put you in touch with your sacred self.

AN ENLIGHTENING MOMENT

✳

As Pisces rules the feet, a 'step forward' on the journey to enlightenment and discovering your sacred self seems the most appropriate way to start.

But what is enlightenment, anyway? This experience is very personal to us all: you might suddenly feel 'at one with the Universe'; it's an epiphany moment, when everything falls into place, you know who you really are, where you are going, your purpose and your true intentions. A sort of 'Ah-yes, of-course!' moment, with a deeper sense of peace and acceptance. However you experience this, the following practice will take you there, and help you to discover this stepping stone on your own spiritual journey.

According to legend, the Buddha left his footprint on the stony ground on which he stepped just after his own moment of enlightenment. There are many depictions of this footprint in Buddhist temples, known as a *buddhapada*.

You will need:
* A crystal of your choice (one that you are happy to leave in Nature)

1. Go out into the countryside, to a sandy beach or anywhere you can make a good 'footprint' (even in your own green space).

2. When you have found a suitable spot and feel ready, take off your shoes (assuming you haven't already walked a little barefoot) and be aware of your feet, heels, soles and toes as they press into the ground.

3. Purposefully place your foot down into the sand/earth/ground. Be aware of the ground; be aware of your foot and the print you are making. Don't wiggle your toes – just experience the sense of connection to planet Earth.

4. Stay in this position for a minute or so and say:
> Every step I take on this pathway to knowing my sacred self or for a life-changing revelation is because of the potential within myself to make my own spiritual footprint. If not in this moment, I will very soon know the Way.

5. Lift your foot from the ground and place the crystal on the print you have made, and press it into the earth/sand. Finally, cover both the print and the crystal with more earth/sand to seal your intention for an epiphany experience.

Leave your petition and walk away, knowing you are taking the step forward to personal enlightenment.

....

FOR SPIRITUAL STRENGTH

＊

It's all very well for Pisces to get spiritually connected, but because they are very open to the flow of all kinds of psychic energies, both good and not so good, they can get swept away on a wave of idealism.

The lotus has come to symbolise spiritual attainment in many Eastern belief systems.

Growing from the dark, muddy bottom of a pond, it pushes its way up to the light, then, once above the surface of the water, its petals unfold. The flower's growth represents the struggle Pisceans have with facing their own demons and muddy waters, as they grow towards spiritual awareness and the light. You, too, can unfold and open yourself to the divine with this protective force alongside you.

This little practice will promote spiritual strength and grounding.

You will need:
* A teaspoon of rose water
* A glass bowl of spring water
* A real or imitation lotus flower

1. Add the rose water to your spring water, and gently swirl your finger in an anticlockwise direction.

2. Place your flower gently on the water's surface and focus on your spiritual intentions and your desire to be safe from psychic negativity.

3. After a minute or so, take the flower and gently place it on a high shelf or ledge, where it won't be disturbed.

Leave the lotus for one lunar cycle to promote not only deeper awareness, but also spiritual belief in your Pisces soul.

....

THE SHOAL–OF–FISH VISUALISATION

♡

Understanding human nature is, for Pisceans, both a gift and a curse (being at the mercy of the dark emotions of others), who 'feel' all there is to be felt in the world. Perform this simple visualisation to feel connected to humanity, but also separate enough from any invasive undercurrents. Then you will find stillness in your own sacred self.

1. Visualise a shoal of fish swimming as one in the ocean, always moving forwards in search of sustenance to survive. This is like humanity, all bound together by a common destiny – that of living on this Earth, hopefully loving this planet, forever moving forwards, hungry for answers to life and the Universe.

Imagine now that you are just one of the thousands of fish in the shoal, as you slip through the oceans of life on your quest for self-understanding. Imagine all the other fish in the sea around you, and how they too are all on their own personal journeys. You are never completely alone in the sea of humanity, yet you are also individual and autonomous and have a deep connection to the collective shoal and the divine that flows through everything.

2. Come out of your visualisation and enjoy opening your eyes to the world.

Realise that you are part of the shoal, but separate and unique, too, and give thanks to the spiritual light that shines through every one of us. It's shining through you now.

Last Words

For Pisceans, self-care is about finding joy in mind, body and soul, so that the Fish can feel personally fulfilled but still help the people they care about. Although caring for others means you have often lost out on caring for yourself, this book has given you a range of practices and rituals to restore your sense of ego and individuality. It also shows you how to be uplifted by your own creativity and beliefs, rather than passively accepting what others think is right for you. You can now say, 'Hey, it's all right to be me, and I have an identity all my own', as you take that step towards self-containment.

You've also seen that low self-esteem and self-sacrifice can be augmented to self-empowerment and self-belief. You no longer need to give your all in every relationship to find love. In fact, self-care means loving yourself first, so you can be loved for who and what you truly are – enigmatic, elusive, mysterious and, above all, filled with heartfelt compassion.

More than anything, Pisceans need to find a layer of protection against the pain of the outside world, and also to accept their need for change, their restless nature and their romance with life itself. With this in mind, self-care for you is a sanctuary for mind, body and soul, and it's also about finding a role or profession (among the many you identify with) to nurture and protect you from the currents of life, while, paradoxically, going with the flow.

You may become the wise counsellor, who uses her instinctive wisdom to help others. Or the archetypal good witch, who combines natural magic with her profound awareness of the Universe and people's needs. Because for you, Pisces, it's not about donning your cloak of many colours to escape with the fairies, but finding the true essence of yourself and your solar potential. Knowing who Pisces really is means you are caring about who you are becoming. Let the light of the Universe shine through you every day and, in so doing, know that in your heart and soul you are loved not only by the cosmos, but also by you.

Resources

Main sites for crystals, stones, candles, smudging sticks, incense, pouches, essential oils and everything needed for the holistic self-care practices included in this book:
holisticshop.co.uk
thepsychictree.co.uk
thesoulangels.co.uk
earthcrystals.com
livrocks.com
artisanaromatics.com

For a substantial range of books (and metaphysical items) on astrology, divination, runes, palmistry, tarot and holistic health, etc.:
thelondonastrologyshop.com
watkinsbooks.com
mysteries.co.uk
barnesandnoble.com
innertraditions.com

For more information on astrology, personal horo-scopes and birth-chart calculations:
astro-charts.com (simplest, very user friendly)

horoscopes.astro-seek.com
(straightforward)
astrolibrary.org/free-birth-chart
(easy to use, with lots of extra information)

Glossary

Aura An invisible electromagnetic energy field that emanates from and surrounds all living beings

Auric power The dominant colour of the aura that reveals your current mood or state

Chakra Sanskrit for 'wheel', in Eastern spiritual traditions, the seven chakras are the main epicentres – or wheels – of invisible energy throughout the body

Dark of the moon This is when the moon is invisible to us, due to its proximity to the sun; it is a time for reflection, solitude and a deeper awareness of oneself

Divination Gaining insight into the past, present and future using symbolic or esoteric means

Double-terminator crystal A quartz crystal with a point at each end, allowing its energy to flow both ways

Full moon The sun is at its maximum opposition to the moon, thus casting light across all of the moon's orb; in esoteric terms, it is a time for culmination, finalising deals, committing to love and so on

Geopathic stress Negative energy emanating from and on the Earth, such as underground water courses, tunnels, overhead electrical cables and geological faults

Grid A specific pattern or layout of items symbolising specific intentions or desires

Horoscope An astrological chart or diagram showing the position of the sun, moon and planets at the time of any given event, such as the moment of somebody's birth, a marriage or the creation of an enterprise; it is used to interpret the characteristics or to forecast the future of that person or event

New crescent moon A fine sliver of crescent light that appears curving outwards to the right in the northern hemisphere and to the left in the southern hemisphere; this phase is for beginning new projects, new romance, ideas and so on

Psychic energy One's intuition, sixth sense or instincts, as well as the divine, numinous or magical power that flows through everything

Shadow side In astrology, your shadow side describes those aspects of your personality associated with your opposite sign and of which you are not usually aware

Smudging Clearing negative energy from the home with a smouldering bunch of dried herbs, such as sage

Solar return salutation A way to give thanks and welcome the sun's return to your zodiac sign once a year (your birthday month)

Sun in opposition The sun as it moves through the opposite sign to your own sun sign

Sun sign The zodiac sign through which the sun was moving at the exact moment of your birth

Waning moon The phase of the moon after it is full, when it begins to lose its luminosity – the waning moon is illuminated on its left side in the northern hemisphere, and on its right side in the southern hemisphere; this is a time for letting go, acceptance and preparing to start again

Waxing moon The phase between a new and a full moon, when it grows in luminosity – the waxing moon is illuminated on its right side in the northern hemisphere and on its left side in the southern hemisphere; this is a time for putting ideas and desires into practice

Zodiac The band of sky divided into twelve segments (known as the astrological signs), along which the paths of the sun, the moon and the planets appear to move

About the Author

After studying at the Faculty of Astrological Studies in London, the UK, Sarah gained the Diploma in Psychological Astrology – an in-depth 3-year professional training programme cross-fertilised by the fields of astrology and depth, humanistic and transpersonal psychology. She has worked extensively in the media as astrologer for titles such as *Cosmopolitan* magazine (UK), *SHE, Spirit & Destiny* and the *London Evening Standard*, and appeared on UK TV and radio shows, including *Steve Wright in the Afternoon* on BBC Radio 2.

Her mainstream mind-body-spirit books include the international bestsellers, *The Tarot Bible, The Little Book of Practical Magic* and *Secrets of the Universe in 100 Symbols*.

Sarah currently practises and teaches astrology and other esoteric arts in the heart of the countryside.

Acknowledgements

I would first like to thank everyone at Yellow Kite, Hodder & Stoughton and Hachette UK who were part of the process of creating this series of twelve zodiac self-care books. I am especially grateful to Carolyn Thorne for the opportunity to write these guides; Anne Newman for her editorial advice, which kept me 'carefully' on the right track; and Olivia Nightingall who kept me on target for everything else! It is when people come together with their different skills and talents that the best books are made – so I am truly grateful for being part of this team.